100 QUESTIONS AND A[illegible]

PONIES AND HORSES

Written by
Jenny Millington

Consultant
Elwyn Hartley Edwards

CHRYSALIS CHILDREN'S BOOKS

Jenny Millington, the author, is an experienced horsewoman who has her own horse, and regularly competes at shows and hunter trials. Jenny is a freelance writer and editor, working mainly on children's information books.

Elwyn Hartley Edwards has written and edited over 50 books and is an authority on a wide variety of equestrian subjects. He has worked to promote the Riding for the Disabled Association, and teaches riding and judges horses.

This edition published in 2003 by Big Fish, an imprint of Chrysalis Children's Books.

Printed in Thailand by Imago

ISBN 1 84347 0 74 8

Editorial Director: Honor Head
Senior Editor: Sarah Walker
Design by Grand Union Design
Illustrations: Peter Dennis, Maureen Gray, Richard Berridge, Gerry Wood and John Yates.

Contents

About this book

Ponies and horses are beautiful creatures. Discover when and where they first lived and how they evolved over hundreds of years. Find out about the kind of horses and ponies you can ride and the equipment you need.

Do you know what a gymkhana is and how to take part? Or, which sports involve horses and how horses are trained? Have you got the right clothes for riding and when do you need to groom your pony? There are many questions you will want to ask and you'll find lots of the answers on the pages that follow.

If you can't wait to start riding or if you own a pony already, you will enjoy the exciting and colourful pictures and find that this book is packed with fascinating information all about your favourite animals!

A foal can walk and follow its mother just an hour after it has been born.

How do ponies and horses differ?

A pony is a small horse – one that is less than 14.2 hands high. Ponies and horses are traditionally measured in hands and inches (see page 11). One hand is equal to 10.16 cm (4 in).

Q Which is the heaviest breed of horse?

A The Shire horse is the world's largest and heaviest breed. Shires are usually about 17.2 hands high (178 cm/70 in) and weigh about 1 tonne (1 ton). They are working horses and are still used in cities to pull heavy loads such as brewers' drays or carts. They also work in the forestry industry, dragging felled trees in the forest.

Q How small is the smallest horse?

A The Falabella is a miniature breed of horse measuring no more than 76 cm (30 in) or 7 hands 2 inches! They are about as big as a medium-sized dog and are kept as pets, not used for riding. Next smallest are the Shetland ponies, whose average height is 1 metre (40in).

Q Do horses need companionship?

A All horses and ponies are herd animals – in the wild they live in large groups and depend on each other for company and protection. Domesticated horses and ponies become very attached to each other or their human owners. If there are no other horses nearby, they will often form close friendships with other animals, such as goats, or even cats and dogs.

Standing among the giants of the Shire horse breed is 'King' who stood at 19.2 hands (198 cm/78 in).

Shetland ponies are traditionally measured in inches, not hands.

Q Which type of horse is the fastest?

A Thoroughbred horses are the fastest horses in the world. They are bred especially for racing and are both strong and lightweight. All Thoroughbreds are descended from three famous stallions that were brought to Britain from North Africa in the early 1700s - the Byerley Turk, the Darley Arabian and the Godolphin Barb.

Q How do you breed a mule?

A A mule is the offspring (foal) of a male donkey (jackass) and a female horse (mare). Mules are very strong and sure-footed, so they are often used as pack animals to carry heavy loads over uneven country. Mules are always sterile, which means they cannot produce foals of their own.

Q Can ponies be ridden by adults?

A Most native British breeds, such as Exmoor, Fell and New Forest ponies, can be ridden by adults, but most modern 'show' type ponies with their thin, fine bodies and legs would probably be too small. The sturdy Highland pony was bred to carry full-grown men over the Scottish moors, even though the riders' feet nearly touched the ground!

Q Is a zebra a type of horse?

A Yes, zebras and horses belong to the same family of mammals, called 'Equidae'. Zebras live in Africa in large herds, and their striped colouring is thought to be a form of camouflage. Some peple have tried to tame and ride zebras, but without much success. They are just too wild.

The earliest horses probably ate shrubby plants and leaves rather than grass.

How did the horse evolve?

Horses evolved gradually over about 55 million years. The earliest horses had more than one toe on each foot, and were much smaller than the modern animal. As the horse evolved, the foot became a hoof, which is really a single toe, and the size of the animal increased.

Q What did the first horse look like?

A The earliest known ancestor of the horse was called *Eohippus*, which means 'dawn horse'. It was about the size of a fox, and had four toes on its front feet and three on its hind feet. It is thought that *Eohippus* weighed only about 5.4 kg (12 lb) and may have had a mottled coat, like a deer's coat, for camouflage in the forests where it lived.

Q How do we know about early horses?

A Fossil remains of horses at different stages of their evolution have been found in many places. A complete skeleton of *Eohippus* was found in 1867 in the southern part of America, and parts of a skull were found in south-east England in 1920.

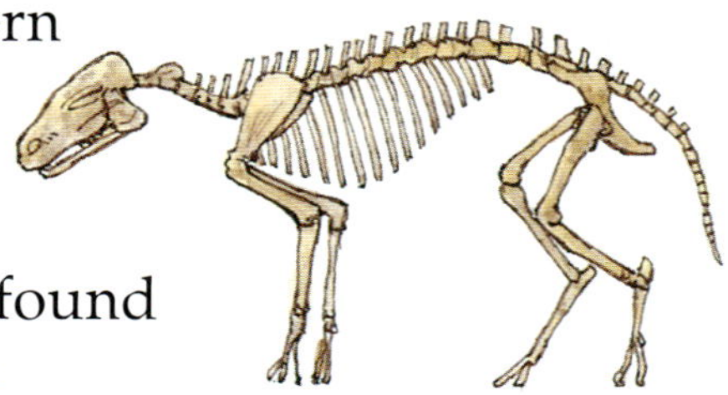

Q Where did horses originally come from?

A *Eohippus* is thought to have lived first in North America, and then to have spread to Europe, Asia and Africa while these lands were joined together over 50 million years ago. Strangely, the horse became extinct in America 10,000 years ago in the Ice Age – no one knows for certain why this happened. Spanish invaders re-introduced horses to America in the 16th century.

This painting on a wall of the Lascaux caves in France could be 15,000 years old.

In 1890, there were 300,000 horses living and working in London.

Nomadic tribes in Central Asia made a drink called Kummis, from mares' milk.

Q What kinds of work have horses done?

A Until the steam engine was invented in the 1820's, the horse was the main form of transport for people and goods. Farm work, such as ploughing, was carried out using horses until earlier this century, and thousands of ponies worked in the mines pulling coal tubs. People travelled around in horse-drawn carts and carriages.

Q When were horses first domesticated?

A Horses were probably first kept as domestic animals in the Ukraine, near the Black sea, about 6000 years ago. The people of the Steppe lands were nomadic, moving their homes and herding animals from place to place throughout the year. Horses were bred to be ridden, for milk and for meat.

Q Are there any wild horses left in the world?

A The last truly wild horses lived in Mongolia in eastern Asia until the 1960s when they were hunted almost to extinction. Some 50 specimens of these Przewalski horses are believed to exist in the wild, though 200 are being carefully bred in zoos. They were named Przewalski horses after the man who discovered them in 1881.

Q Have horses always gone to war?

A The Ancient Egyptians and Greeks used horse-drawn war chariots, and medieval knights rode to battle on horseback. Even up to World War II (1939-1945) many horses were used to pull guns and equipment and as mounts for soldiers, called cavalry.

The Arab is the oldest pure breed of horse in the world.

How many breeds are there?

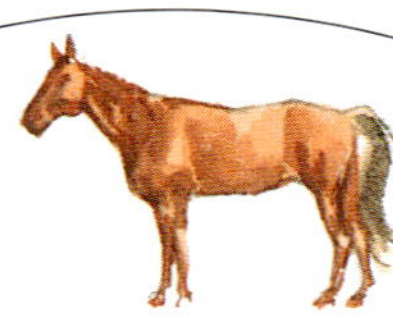

About 200 breeds of horse have been described, more than 60 of which are ponies. However, many of these are cross-breeds (a mixture of two or more types) and no one knows the exact total.

Q Why are there different breeds?

A When horses lived in the wild they gradually adapted to their surroundings. For example, in the mountains they became small and sure-footed. After the horse was domesticated people deliberately bred horses to suit the work they were required to do. Large, strong animals were bred for heavy work and lighter, faster ones for riding.

Q What are cobs used for?

A Cobs are 'all-round' horses, good-natured enough to be ridden by children, and sturdy enough to carry adults. The cob is a type of horse rather than a breed – they are often a cross between a light-weight and a heavier horse. Their manes are almost always 'hogged' (clipped right off) to show off their powerful neck and shoulders.

Q What is an Appaloosa?

A The Appaloosa is an American breed of horse with a spotted coat. It was first bred by the Nez Percé Amerindians, and its name comes from the Palouse river territory where they lived. Appaloosas have been very popular as circus horses because of their attractive coats.

A fleabitten grey horse has a white coat with small brown flecks.

A horse that is just ridden for pleasure is called a 'hack'.

The horses of the Camargue, in southern France, live in the wet lands of the Rhone delta. They have wide, hard hooves for living in the marshes.

Q What is the difference between a piebald and a skewbald?

A A piebald horse has a white coat with large irregular patches of black. Skewbald is the name for a horse with large patches of white on any coat apart from black.

Q Is a palomino a breed of horse?

A No, palomino refers to a particular colour of a horse's or pony's coat, mane and tail. The coat is a light or rich golden colour, and the mane and tail are white. Ideally, a palomino shouldn't have any black hair.

Q What are the markings on a horse's face called?

A White patches of hair often occur on the face, and the patterns have different names. A small patch on the forehead is called a 'star' and a thin white strip is called a 'stripe'. A wide white mark running down the face is a 'blaze', and a small white patch on the end of the nose is known as a 'snip'.

Q Do horses ever change colour?

A Once a horse or pony is mature, its colour usually stays the same for the rest of its life. However, the colour of a foal can change as it grows up. Lipizzaner horses are usually grey (the proper term for a white horse) but their foals are born with black coats. If a horse's coat is damaged by an injury, the hair will often grow back white.

Long hairs on the fetlocks of some breeds are called 'feather'.

What are the points of a horse?

The picture on these pages shows the main points of a horse. The term 'points' refers to all the proper names for the different parts of a horse's body.

Q Why is conformation important?

A Conformation is the proper term for the overall shape and size of a horse's body and legs. A horse has good conformation when everything is in proportion. Bad conformation, such as a dipped back, can lead to health problems.

Q When does a horse 'forge'?

A 'Forging' can happen when the horse is walking or trotting. The hind foot strikes the underside of the front foot, making a loud crack.

Q Where is the frog?

A On the underside of the hoof. It is the triangular, rubbery section that runs from the heel to roughly the centre of the sole. It acts as a kind of pump to regulate the blood supply to the horse's foot and lower leg. If the horse is standing on a soft surface, the frog may touch the ground.

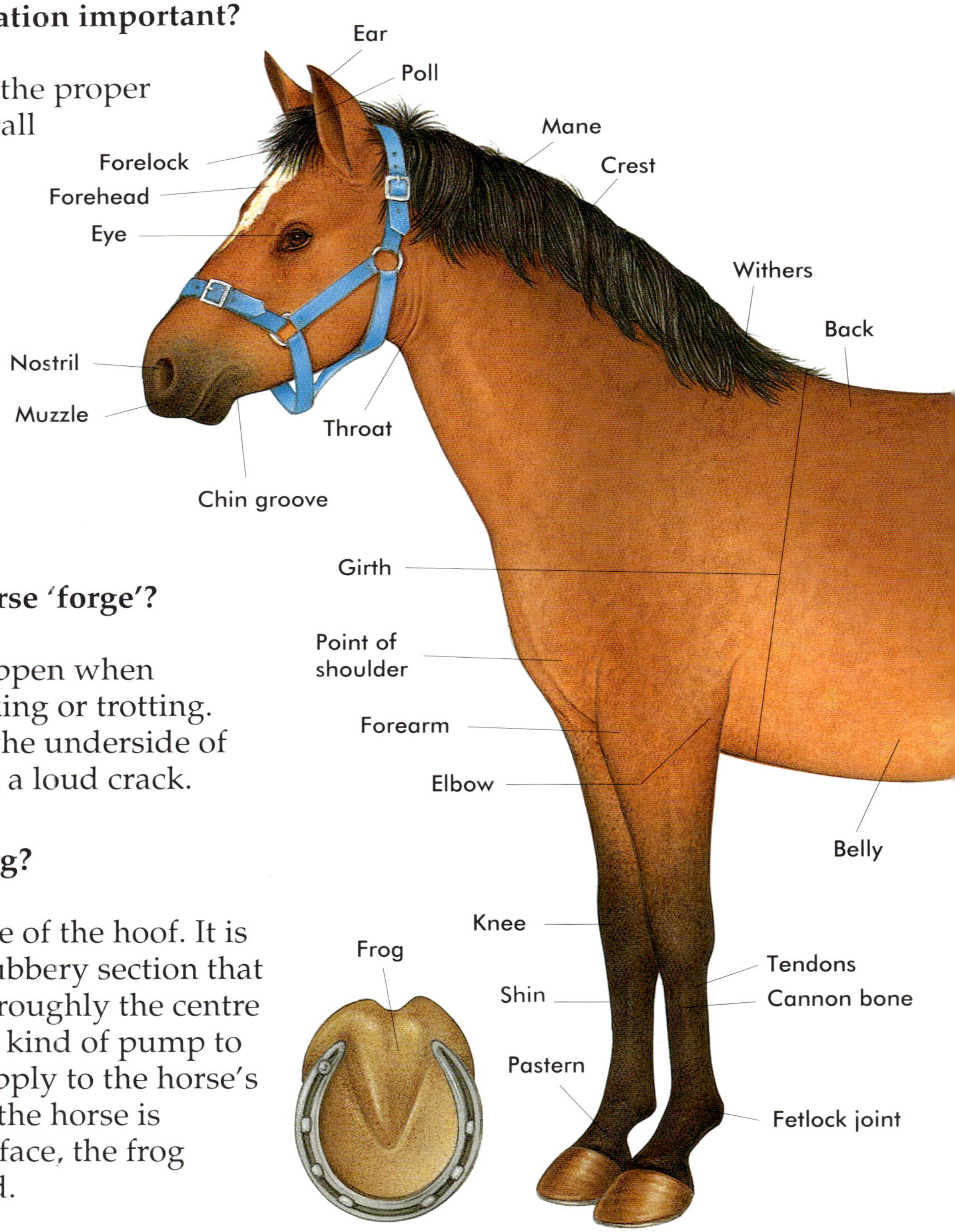

A mature male horse has 36 teeth plus 4 tushes (small pointed teeth). Mares do not usually have tushes.

Ponies and horses can live for over 30 years.

Q How do you tell a horse's age?

A The most usual way is by looking at the teeth. Because ponies' and horses' teeth grow and wear down throughout their lives, you can estimate an animal's age by the amount of wear and the length of the front teeth, called incisors.

Q What is 'dishing'?

A When a horse or pony's front legs swing outwards as it moves forward, the animal is said to 'dish'.

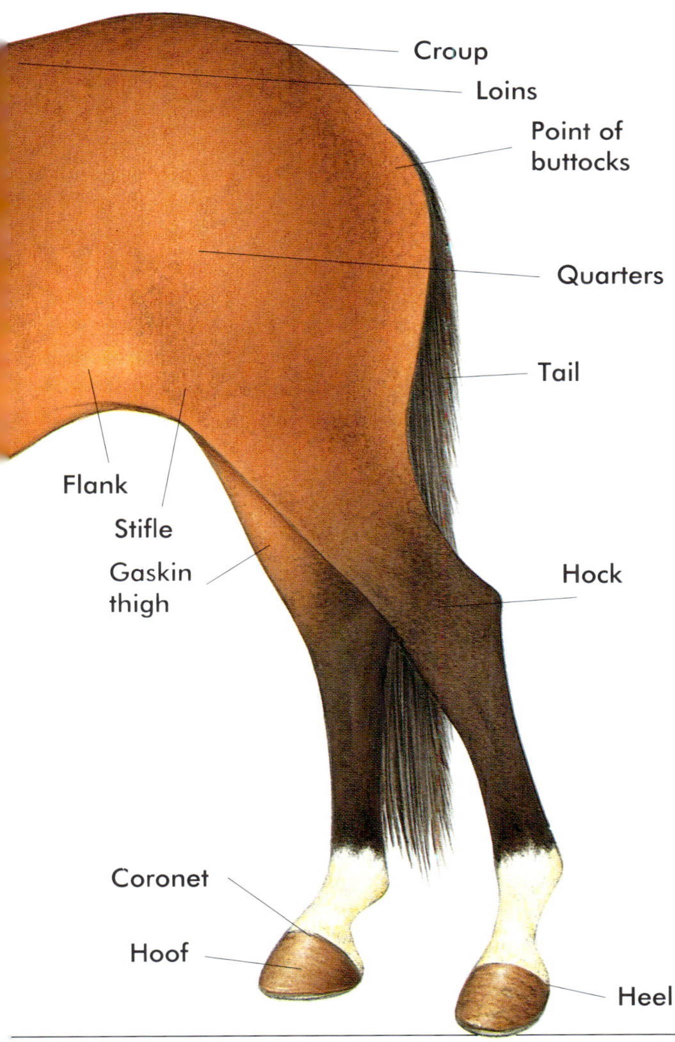

Q How many gaits do horses have?

A There are four natural gaits – walk, trot, canter and gallop. The walk and gallop have four beats (1-2-3-4); the trot has two beats (1-2, 1-2); and the canter has three beats (1-2-3, 1-2-3).

Q Why are horses measured in hands?

A A hand is 10.16 cm (4 inches) – about the width of a man's hand across the palm. Before tape measures were used, people who bought and sold horses measured a horse's height, to the top of the withers, by placing their hands one on top of the other.

Horses greet each other by blowing into each other's nostrils.

How are horses trained?

Horses are trained over a fairly long period by carefully introducing new experiences one at a time. Most horses and ponies are actually quite willing to learn and eager to please.

Q How early can you start to train a horse?

A At only one week old, a foal can learn to wear a small headcollar and to trust humans to stroke and handle it. Making an early start like this will help when the horse is old enough to be broken in and ridden.

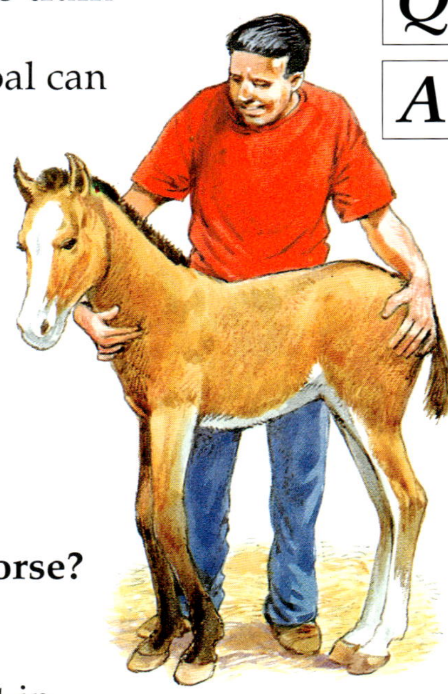

Q How long does it take to train a horse?

A Training really continues throughout a horse's life. There is always something new to learn, whatever sport or job the horse is used for.

Q How do you break in a horse?

A Once a horse is used to wearing a bridle with a bit in its mouth, you can lay a saddle cloth across the horse's back. Next comes the saddle, but without a girth. Then the girth is added and gradually tightened. After a while, the horse will learn to carry the weight of a person, at first leaning over its back, and later on, sitting in the saddle.

Laid-back ears mean an aggressive or angry horse.

Horses sometimes curl their upper lips if they taste something strong or unusual.

Q What is lungeing?

A A long rein, called a lunge rein, is used so that the horse can move round its trainer in a circle. The trainer gives commands such as 'Walk on!' and 'Trot!'. Later, the horse is lunged with a rider on its back, and learns to respond to commands from the rider's legs and hands as well as the voice.

Q Do horses have to be taught to jump?

A Horses and ponies will jump things naturally, but they do not often bother to do so, or they would always be escaping from their fields. They do have to be taught to jump neatly with the weight of a rider on their backs.

Q What does a racing trainer do?

A People who train racehorses must keep them in perfect health, and make sure they are fit and full of energy on the day of a race. A horse's herd instinct makes it gallop with other horses, so trainers develop this natural urge during training.

Q Are horses' senses sharper than humans' senses?

A Horses can see and hear much more than humans can, and their sense of smell is many times keener. In the wild, horses needed sharp senses to detect danger in time to escape.

Q Do police horses have special training?

A Yes, police horses learn to stay calm when surrounded by crowds of noisy people, for example at football matches. A horse's natural reaction would be to run away.

A 'Dr Bristol' is a type of snaffle bit with a jointed plate in the middle.

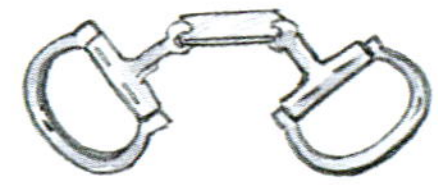

What equipment do you need to ride?

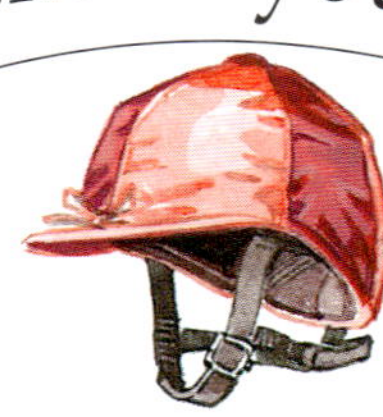

The most important piece of equipment for the rider is a hard riding hat, and you should never ride without one. Most riding schools will lend you a hat when you first start learning to ride.

Q What kind of clothes should you wear?

A As well as a hard hat you will need boots or shoes with a 1.5 cm heel – trainers or wellingtons are not a good idea as they can get stuck in the stirrups. Jodhpurs are tight-fitting trousers specially made for riding with extra material inside the knees, but tough leggings or comfortable stretch jeans will do instead.

Q Why does a horse need a bit?

A The metal bit rests in the horse's mouth in a gap between the front and back teeth, and helps the rider to steer and control the horse. The most common type of bit is called a snaffle. Strong horses may need a different type, such as a curb bit.

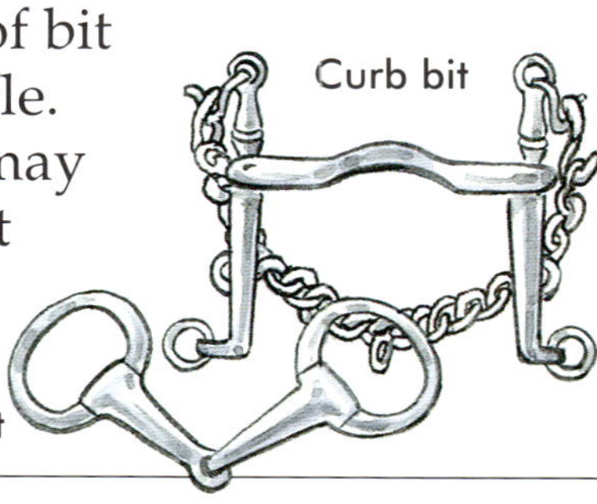

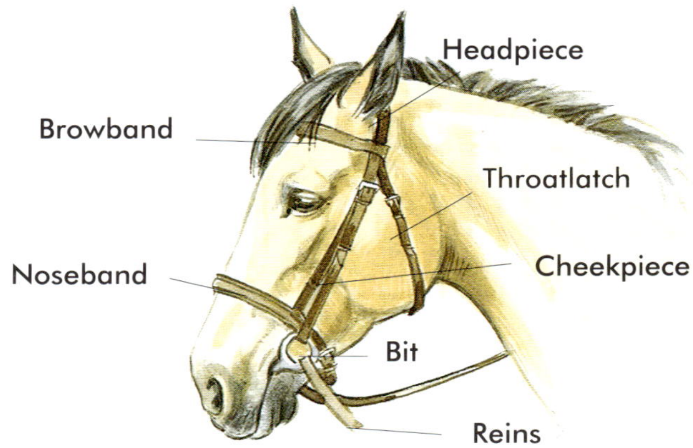

Q What are the parts of a bridle called?

A The diagram above shows a bridle with the names of all the different straps. It is very important to adjust the bridle until it fits the horse or pony perfectly. The proper name for the bridle and saddle is 'tack'.

The pad or cloth worn under the saddle is called a numnah.

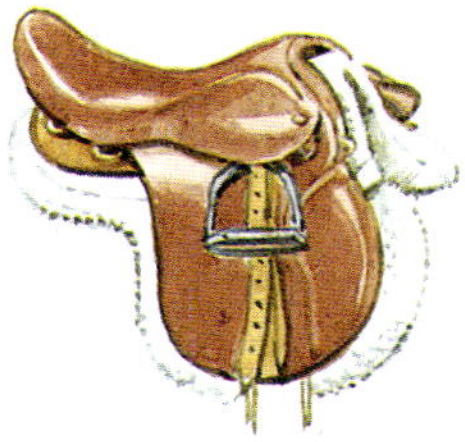

Many riders wear brightly coloured, reflective clothing so that they can ride safely on the road.

What is a hackamore?

Some horses cannot wear a bit in their mouths, perhaps because of an injury. Instead, they might be ridden in a hackamore (as below), which is a special bridle that has no bit. The long cheeks of the hackamore act like levers on the noseband to control the horse.

How often should tack be cleaned?

Ideally, you should clean your tack after every ride, but if you don't have time, then a tack-cleaning session once a week is a good idea. Clean, supple leather will last longer and be less likely to break.

What is the right way to put on a bridle?

First, put the reins over the horse's head. Then hold the headpiece in your right hand and the bit in your left hand. Open the horse's mouth by gently sliding your thumb into the corner. Slip the bit into the horse's mouth and bring the headpiece up over the ears. Make sure everything is comfortably in place, then fasten the noseband and the throatlatch.

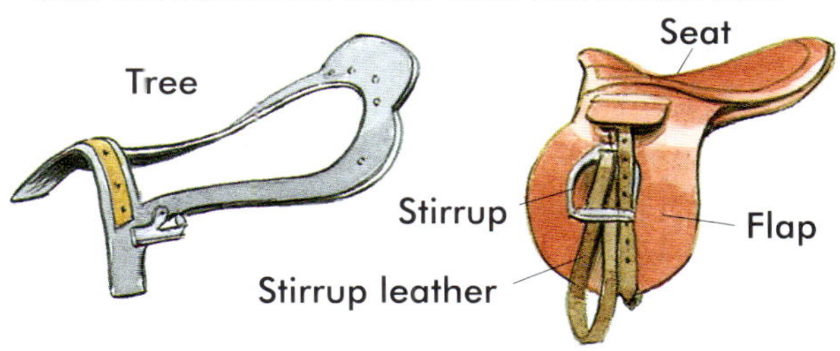

How is a saddle made?

The inner framework of the saddle, called the 'tree', is made of lightweight wood. The bars that hold the stirrup leathers are fixed to this. The seat of the saddle is built up around the tree, over webbing, and the flaps sewn on. A wool-stuffed panel is added to the underside so that the saddle lies comfortably on the horse's back.

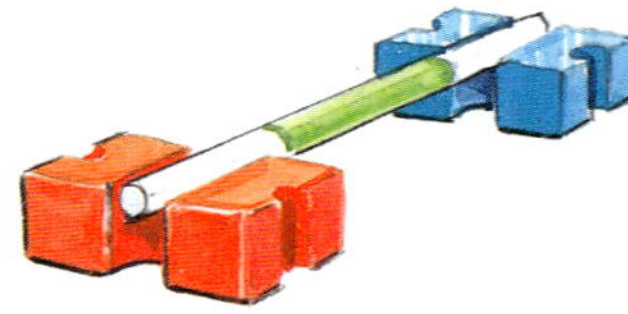

Small jumps used in lessons are sometimes called 'cavalletti'.

How do you learn to ride?

The best way to learn to ride is to go to a registered riding school and have lessons. A qualified instructor will gradually teach you all the different skills.

Q What will the first lesson be like?

A The first thing you need to learn is the correct way to get on to the horse, how to sit properly and how to hold the reins. Your first lesson might be on the lunge rein (see page 13) so that you can learn to balance without having to steer the horse as well.

Q What is the most difficult thing to learn?

A A tricky question! It can take some time to learn to sit up straight and not to pull on the reins to keep your balance. Some people find trot and canter hard work at first. Riding is fun to learn, but it involves thinking about several different things at once, and you will need patience.

Q What is rising trot?

A The most comfortable way to ride in trot is to lift your weight out of the saddle on each alternate step – up on step one, down on step two, up again on step three and so on. You need to learn to do this without bouncing up and down too much.

Rising trot used to be called 'posting' because it was first practised by mounted post-boys.

Mounted exercises during a lesson will improve your balance, position and confidence.

Q How do you learn to jump?

A First, you need to shorten your stirrups by one or two holes, so that your knees and ankles can act as 'shock absorbers' as you go over the jump. Then you learn to fold your body forwards from the waist, first while riding over trotting poles, then over small jumps.

Q What are the 'aids'?

A All the different ways in which a rider controls a horse are known as the 'aids'. The main ones are pressure on the horse's sides with your legs, gentle contact on the reins, your weight in the saddle and your voice. Horses are trained to recognise special patterns of aids that tell them what to do.

Q How soon can you go out for a ride?

A When you are first learning to ride, it is safer to be led, either by someone walking alongside or by another rider. Once you can control your horse or pony yourself, and you feel confident enough, you can begin to enjoy riding in the countryside.

Q What are trotting poles?

A Riding over trotting poles is the first stage in learning to jump. The poles are laid out on the ground, carefully spaced so that the horse can trot over them while you learn the correct position in the saddle for jumping. Later, the last pole in the line will be replaced by a small jump.

Q How do you canter and gallop?

A Canter is a fast rocking movement. Once you have learned to ask a horse to canter, you need to practise sitting quietly in the saddle. When a horse is galloping, the rider's weight is almost always lifted out of the saddle and the body leaning slightly forward.

Although horses love mints and sugar lumps, they are very bad for their teeth!

How do you choose a pony?

It is best not to decide on the first pony you see – look at as many as you can and try them out. Choose one that is the right size and temperament for you.

Q Where should you keep a pony?

A Ponies and horses can either be kept out in fields, or they can live in stables all the time. A good compromise is to leave them in the field all day and bring them into the stable at night, especially in the winter.

Q What equipment do you need to keep a stable tidy?

A To muck out a stable bed you will need a four-tined fork for straw beds, or a shavings fork for wood shavings or paper. You will also need a shovel, a wheelbarrow to take the wet bedding to the muck heap, and a broom to sweep up afterwards.

Horses' hooves must be picked out every day to remove mud and dirt.

Fescue, rye and timothy are all types of grass eaten by horses

Q What do horses eat?

A A horse's natural diet is grass, which is also fed to them dried as hay. Horses that are working or being ridden are also given grains, such as oats, maize or barley, to keep them fit. You can buy ready-mixed horse or pony food which contains all the right ingredients for good health. Carrots and apples are good for horses too.

Q What do horses need for bedding?

A Stable beds can be made of straw or wood shavings, or even shredded paper! The bed must be kept clean and dry, and you should 'muck out' (take out any droppings and wet bedding) at least once a day.

Q Are some plants poisonous to horses?

A Yes, ragwort, deadly nightshade, bracken and yew are all poisonous. You should remove these plants from the field before turning your horse or pony out to graze.

Q What is a New Zealand rug?

A A New Zealand rug is a waterproof coat that is worn by some horses while they are out in the fields in wet weather. It has straps that stop the rug from slipping off.

Q Do you have to ride every day?

A If your pony or horse lives out in a field, then you do not need to ride every day, although you must visit the field daily to check that the horse is healthy and has water to drink. Horses that are stabled do need to be exercised every day.

How do you care for your pony?

You can tell if a horse is cold by feeling its ears.

Looking after a pony properly takes a lot of time. They need to be fed, groomed and exercised regularly and must always have water to drink. Caring for your pony should be part of your daily routine.

Q Why is grooming important?

A Thorough grooming keeps a horse or pony's coat and skin in good condition and free from mud and dried sweat. It is also a good time for you to check for cuts and bumps and other injuries.

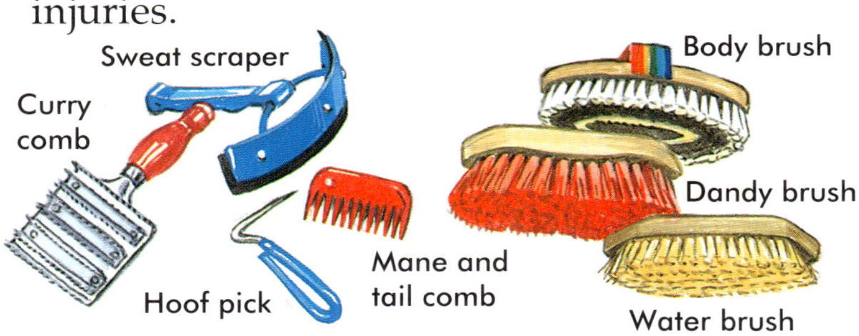

Q What equipment do you need?

A In your grooming kit you will need a stiff dandy brush for removing mud, a soft body brush to make a coat shine, and a water brush for removing difficult stains. Other essential items are a hoofpick, a curry comb, a sweat scraper and a mane and tail comb.

Q How often does a horse need new shoes?

A Horses' hooves are growing all the time, like human fingernails, and horseshoes wear thin as the horse moves around. Every five or six weeks the old shoes should be taken off, the hooves trimmed and new shoes nailed on. This job is done by a specialist called a farrier.

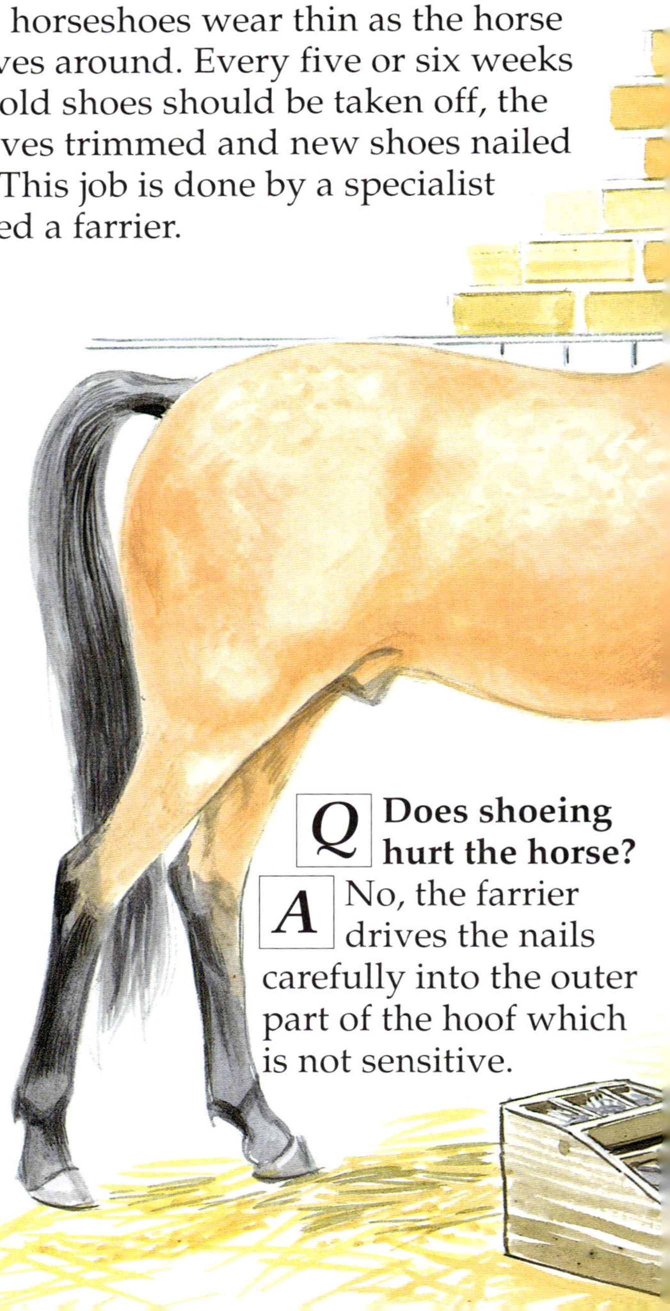

Q Does shoeing hurt the horse?

A No, the farrier drives the nails carefully into the outer part of the hoof which is not sensitive.

A "fullered" shoe has a groove cut into it to give the horse extra grip on the road.

Painting the hooves with special hoof oil helps to keep them healthy.

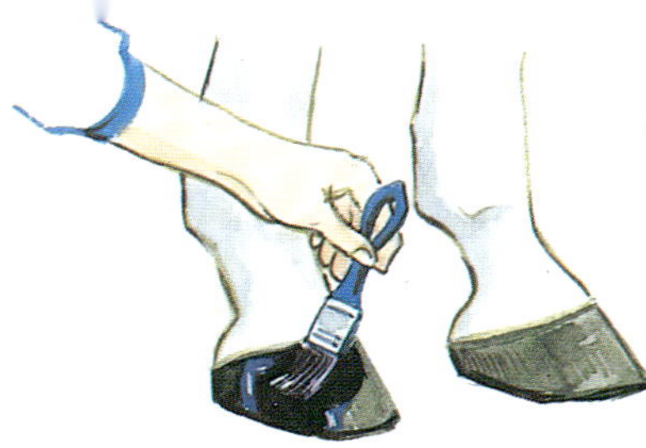

Q When ponies live out all the time, do you still need to groom them?

A Ponies who live out all year round should not be groomed in the winter. Their coats grow long and build up a layer of natural oil that keeps them warm and dry – grooming would remove this. However, you should brush off any mud that lies under the saddle, girth or bridle before you ride.

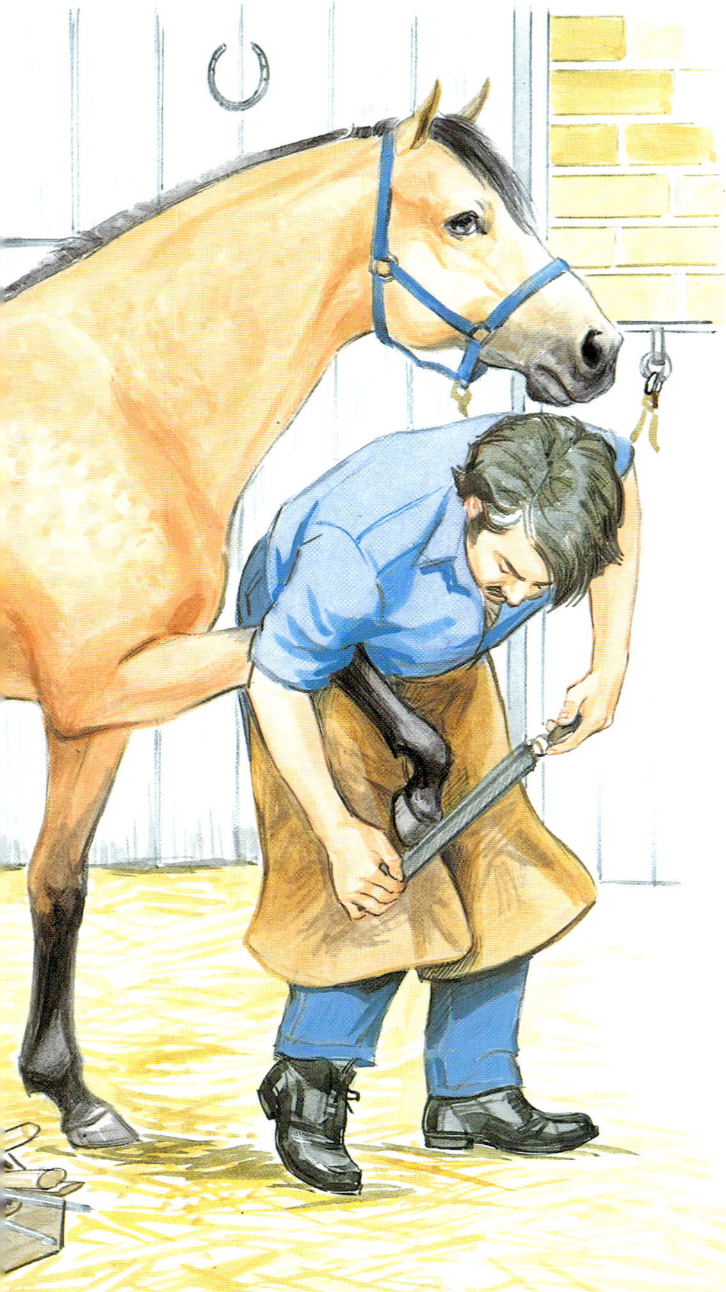

Q Why are some ponies and horses clipped?

A The thick coat that horses grow in winter can make them sweat while they are working or being ridden. To keep them cool and healthy, some horses have part or all of the winter coat clipped off. A clipped horse needs to wear a blanket in the stable and a New Zealand rug out in the field.

Q What is a curry comb for?

A A metal curry comb is used to clear the body brush of hair and dried sweat after every three or four strokes of the brush. Never use a metal curry comb to brush the horse – it is much too sharp. Curry combs made from rubber or plastic can be used to clean mud from the coat.

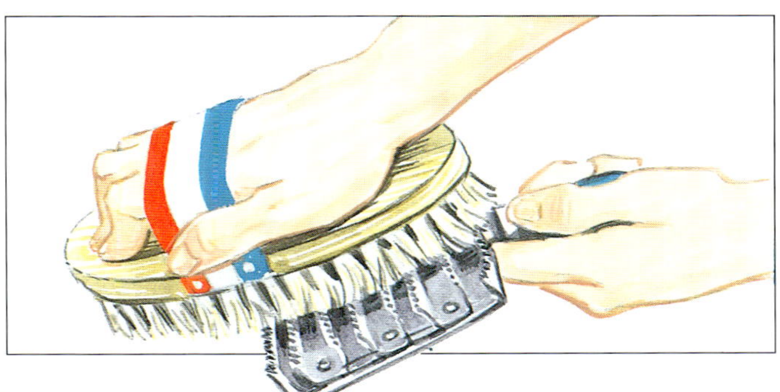

Polo ponies are always called ponies, even though they are usually about 15.2 hands high.

Which sports involve horses?

The Olympic Games include eventing, dressage and show-jumping. Other equestrian sports are racing, polo, long-distance or endurance riding and carriage driving.

Q What is eventing?

A Eventing involves three phases: dressage, cross-country jumping and show-jumping. This is an all round test for both horse and rider. One-day events stage all three phases on the same day, whereas three-day events take place over three (or more usually four) days, and also include a steeplechase course and some timed endurance work called Roads and Tracks.

Q How did steeplechasing begin?

A In 1752, in Ireland, two riders called O'Callaghan and Blake challenged each other to a race between two local churches (from steeple to steeple), jumping hedges along the way. Today, racing over jumps is known as National Hunt racing. The steeplechase phase of a three-day event is run by one horse at a time.

Q How is show-jumping marked?

A Mistakes in the show-jumping ring are marked with 'faults': 4 faults for knocking down a jump and 3 faults for a refusal to jump. Riders are eliminated, or out of the competition, if their horse refuses three times. If the rider falls off, or the horse and rider fall over, they are given 8 faults.

Equestrian sports are unusual because men and women often compete equally against each other.

In 1949, Chilean rider Captain Alberto Morales jumped a staggering 2.44 metres (8ft 1/4in) on a horse called 'Huaso', and set a high-jump record for others to beat.

Q **What are horse-driving trials?**

A These are based on the ridden three-day event trials, but do not, of course, include jumping! In the dressage class the carriage and horses must be driven accurately around a course of narrow obstacles. The marathon is a cross-country drive through woods, water and other hazards. Finally, the carriage, horses and driver are judged for smartness.

Q **Is dressage difficult to learn?**

A Dressage is like equine gymnastics, and is based on the flatwork or skills that riders learn in a riding school. Advanced dressage includes 'lateral work' in which the horse moves sideways as well as forwards. It takes a lot of training before a horse will perform dressage movements perfectly.

Q **What are the 'airs above the ground?'**

A These are a very advanced form of High School riding, usually only performed by specialists such as the Lipizzaners from the Spanish Riding School in Vienna, Austria. The horses are trained to make spectacular leaps and kicks in the air and to rise on their hind legs in a movement called the *levade*.

Q **Where did polo come from?**

A A game like polo, called *changar*, was played in China 2500 years ago. The modern version was taken up by British soldiers serving in India in the 1800s. Polo is played at a gallop and has been described as 'hockey on horseback'.

The Golden Horseshoe Ride takes place every year over 160km (100 miles) of Exmoor in southern Britain.

How do you start competing?

Probably the best way to start competing is to join the Pony Club, which is the junior branch of the British Horse Society. Pony Clubs all over the world organise shows, events and gymkhanas for riders up to the age of twenty-one.

Q Do gymkhana games improve your riding?

A Taking part in mounted games like 'Musical Sacks' and 'Potato Races' will help you to improve your balance and confidence. They also teach you to think ahead and anticipate your pony's every move. These are skills that every rider needs.

Q What is a hunter trial?

A Hunter trials were originally tests for horses and ponies that were used for hunting. These days they are simply cross-country jumping competitions open to everyone. There are usually all kinds of obstacles to jump, such as banks, ditches, and water jumps. It is best to start competing in 'Minimus' classes where the jumps are small (about 53cm/1ft 9in high).

Q Where did the word 'gymkhana' come from?

A During the time when the British ruled India, many Indian words began to be used in the English language. 'Gymkhana' comes from the Hindi word *gendkhana*, which means a place set aside for playing games. 'Jodhpurs' were named after the state of Jodhpur in Rajastan, India.

Bright-coloured shirts, hat covers and body-protectors are usually worn by cross-country competitors.

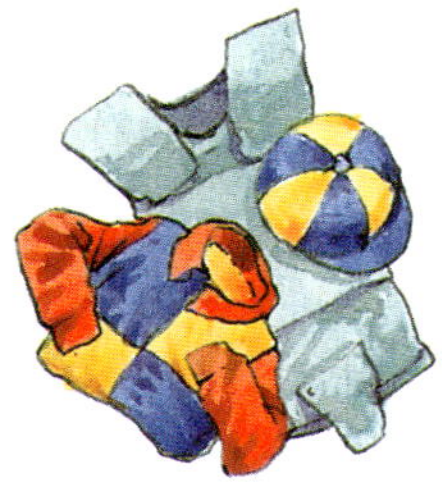

Pony Club Camps last for a week in the summer and provide tuition and fun for riders and their ponies.

Q **Is competing expensive?**

A If you can ride to local shows and hunter trials, competing will cost you very little. However, if you wish to travel further afield, you will need a trailer or horsebox and this can be expensive. Some competitors look for sponsorship, where a company or organisation helps to pay the costs in return for the use of their name for advertising.

Q **What is involved in showing a pony?**

A In showing classes, horses or ponies of the same type or breed are judged on their appearance, that is their shape or conformation and paces. Your pony must be in top condition, and should be bathed and groomed to perfection before the show. Many breeds have their manes and tails plaited for showing classes.

Q **Can anyone do long-distance riding?**

A Yes, as long as you and your horse or pony are very fit and healthy. All over the world there are clubs that organise these events and there are usually two types. Endurance Rides can be up to 160km (100 miles) long and are like races. Trail Rides are ridden at a set speed and there are checkpoints along the way where a vet will see that the horses are fit to continue.

Q **What happens in a ridden showing class?**

A In some showing classes the rider must give an individual display to show the pony at its best, while in 'working' classes for horses and ponies, the rider must jump a course of fences. In an adult ridden show class, the judge rides each horse before choosing a winner.

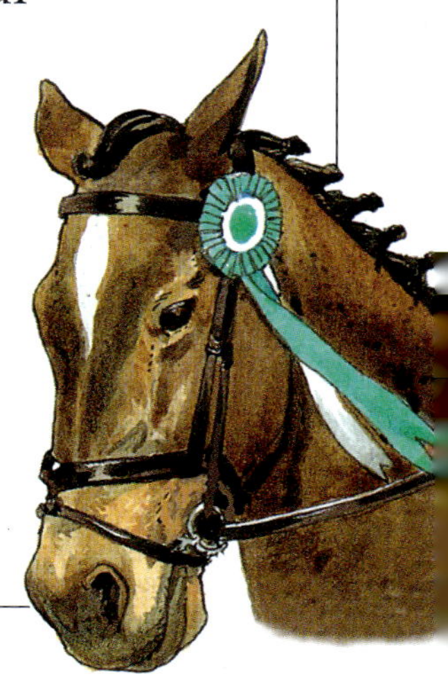

What is Western riding?

In Western riding, trotting is called 'jogging' and cantering called 'loping'.

Western riding came from America and is based on the style of cowboys and cattle ranchers. The clothes, tack and the way of riding are unique. Western riders never rise to the trot and keep their reins very long.

Q How do Western and English saddles differ?

A A Western saddle is heavier than an English one, and has a high horn or pommel at the front. Instead of narrow stirrup-leathers and metal stirrups, a Western saddle has a wide flap, and the broad stirrups are usually made of wood covered with leather.

Q What clothes do Western riders wear?

A Western riding clothes are very different from those worn by European riders. Jeans and chaps (leather over-trousers) are worn with high-heeled boots and a soft, broad-brimmed hat called a Stetson.

Q Do rodeos still take place?

A Yes, all over America there are regular rodeos. Riders test their skills by roping calves, riding broncos (un-broken horses) and 'cutting' cattle, where one animal is separated from the herd and caught by a rider.

American horse shows sometimes have classes for Arab horses whose riders wear Arabian costume.

Until the early 20th century, most women rode side-saddle. Riding astride a horse was considered unladylike.

Q Do women still ride side-saddle?

A Side-saddle riding is very popular in many countries. The rider's legs are held in position by two pommels on the side-saddle. The lower one curved over the left thigh is called the 'leaping head'. Side-saddle riders usually wear long-skirted riding 'habits'.

Q Can you jump while riding side-saddle?

A Because a side-saddle rider is held firmly in position by the curved pommels, jumping is quite safe. Many riders believe that side-saddle is a more secure way to ride.

Q What is a Tennessee Walker?

A A Walker is an American breed of horse. They do not trot, but move from a slow 'flat' walk to a faster 'running' walk that is said to be very comfortable for the rider. These horses are ridden in a distinctive way, with the rider's legs pushed forwards.

Q Is there an Australian ranch horse?

A Horses were first brought to Australia about 200 years ago from South Africa and Europe. They were used to breed the Australian Stock Horse. These are sturdy animals of between 15 and 16.1 hands, and are used for cattle and sheep ranching.

In Greek mythology Apollo rode a winged horse called Pegasus.

Who are the most famous horses?

Throughout history there have been many famous horses, both real and in fiction. Perhaps the earliest famous horse was Bucephalus, a black stallion and the favourite mount of Alexander the Great (356-323 BC).

Q Who is the most well-known horse in fiction?

A This is probably Black Beauty. Anna Sewell wrote *Black Beauty: The Autobiography of a Horse* in 1877, to tell people how badly horses were treated at the time. Since then films and television series based on the Black Beauty stories have been made, and you can still buy the original story today.

Q Why is Desert Orchid so famous?

A The racehorse Desert Orchid, born in 1979, was retired in December 1991 after winning 34 races in his career. His fame was mainly due to his colour, as grey racehorses are unusual, and most do not have as much success as 'Dessie'!

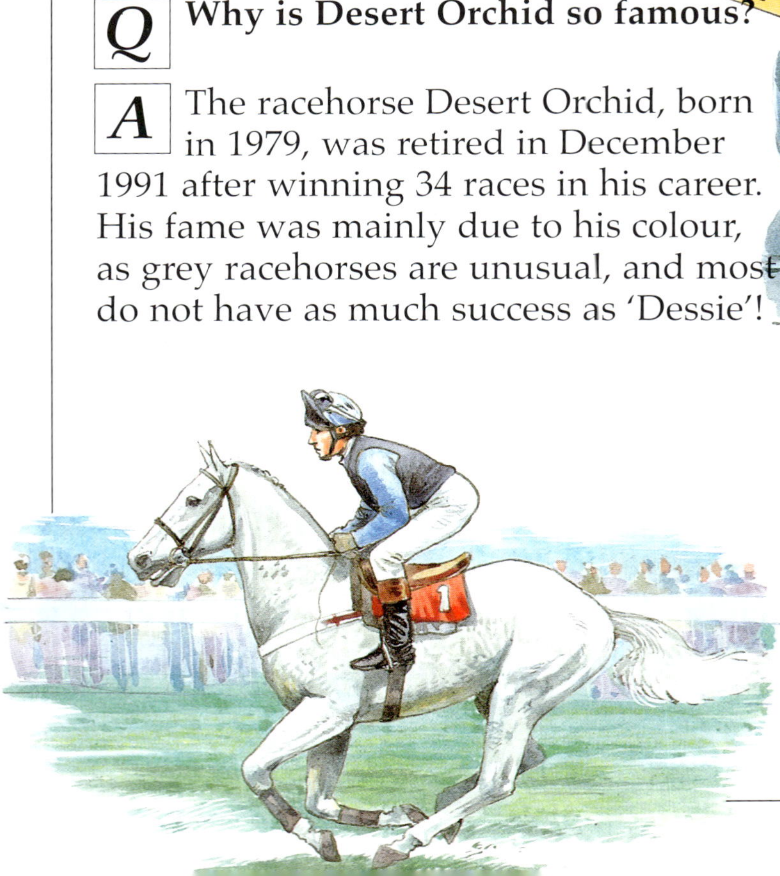

Q What happened to Shergar?

A Shergar was the racehorse who won the Derby in 1981. On 8th February 1983, he was stolen from his stable on a stud farm in Ireland and was never seen again. No-one knows what happened to him.

Emperor Shih Huang-ti of China was buried with 7,500 lifesize models of horses, in 210 BC.

The Princess Royal, Princess Anne, became the first royal lady jockey to win a race in 1982, on a horse called Gulfland.

Q **Who was Marengo?**

A Napoleon's grey charger was called Marengo. He got his name after a battle that took place in 1800 near the village of Marengo in northern Italy, in which Napoleon, Emperor of France, defeated the Austrian forces.

Q **Which horse is known as 'The Golden Horse'?**

A This is another name for the Akhal-Teke, a horse that is bred in the Turkmenistan desert north of Iran. Akhal-Tekes often have unusual-coloured coats that look golden and almost metallic in the sunlight.

Q **Which show-jumper was only a pony?**

A At 14.2 hands high, Stroller was the only internationally successful show-jumping pony. He was ridden by Marion Mould, and together they won the Ladies' World Championship in 1956 and an Olympic silver medal, for the UK, in Mexico in 1968, both times competing against much bigger horses.

Q **Which horse is the most successful show-jumper?**

A Milton, the grey ridden by John Whitaker from the UK, won over £1 million in prize money during his career. When Milton retired in 1994 his winnings were record-breaking.

Where can you work with horses?

A person who makes bits is called a loriner.

There are many careers that involve horses. You could become a riding instructor, or work as a stable hand or groom in an eventing or racing stable. You might ride professionally or train as an equine vet.

Q Can you take exams in riding?

A Yes. The British Horse Society (BHS) sets exams in riding and stable management. The Stage 1 exam covers basic riding skills and knowledge of horse care. You will need to take a Riding and Road Safety test before you can progress to Stages 2, 3, and 4.

Q Is it hard work being a stable hand?

A A stable hand's day begins very early and often ends late. Their duties include feeding, grooming and caring for several horses, as well as mucking out their stables and keeping the yard tidy. Grooms who are good riders exercise the horses every day.

Q Do grooms travel to events with the horses?

A There is a lot of work to be done 'behind the scenes' at all events involving horses. Grooms must prepare the horses for travelling, see that they stay calm in the horsebox and organise all the tack and equipment. They might also exercise the horses before the event begins or lead a racehorse around the paddock before the race.

Stable hands in racing yards are called 'lads' and 'lasses' no matter how old they are.

Farriers serve a four-year apprenticeship with a Master Farrier before they can register with the Worshipful Company of Farriers.

Q **How do you become a riding instructor?**

A You can train to be a BHS riding instructor from the age of sixteen. After passing the Stage 1, 2, and 3 exams you can study for the Preliminary Teaching Test, which will enable you to be an assistant instructor. After that you can take more BHS exams to become a fully qualified instructor.

Q **How long does it take to become an equine vet?**

A It takes five to six years of study to become a veterinary surgeon and then a further two years to specialise in horses. A Registered Animal Nursing Auxiliary (RANA) must study for two years before taking exams, but can work with a vet while still training.

Q **What does a Master Saddler do?**

A Saddlery students spend up to six years learning the craft of saddle, bridle and harness making, both at college and while working with a Master Saddler. Every part of the process is learned – cutting out, shaping and stitching the leather, as well as the skills needed to repair tack.

Q **How do you become a jockey?**

A Trainee jockeys work for racehorse trainers and learn both stable management and riding techniques. They also attend courses at a specialised Racing School. To be a jockey you will need to be brave and small. National Hunt jockeys can weigh up to 76kg (12 stone) but 'flat' racing jockeys, who do not jump, weigh no more than 64kg (10 stone).

Index